THE LITTLE BOOK OF

AGA TIPS

RICHARD MAGGS

THE LITTLE BOOK OF
AGA TIPS

RICHARD MAGGS

A.
Absolute Press

Absolute Press
Scarborough House, 29 James Street West
Bath BA1 2BT, England
Phone 44 (0) 1225 316013 **Fax** 44 (0) 1225 445836
E-mail info@absolutepress.co.uk
Web www.absolutepress.co.uk

First published in Great Britain in 2002
Reprinted 2002, 2003 (twice), 2004

A catalogue record of this book is available
from the British Library

ISBN 1 899791 84 1

Printed and bound in Italy by Lego Print

To Mum and Dad who educated my palate
and taught me to appreciate good food.

1

Invest in **a good**

Aga kettle.

It will boil more quickly than most electric kettles and saves money by using the Aga's stored heat. And, if you place the spout facing the hotplate lid the steam will help keep it clean. Just an occasional wipe will keep it pristine.

2

Place a **lemon** in the roasting oven for three minutes before squeezing to

extract the most juice.

Organic lemons give a far superior flavour and are worth the extra cost.

3

Popcorn

can be **popped**

quite simply on a piece of Bake-O-Glide on the simmering plate, with the lid down. Only pop one tablespoon at a time!

4

Toasted sandwiches

can be made most successfully cooked slowly direct on the simmering plate. Bake-O-Glide may be used but is not essential. Lower the lid and allow 3-4 minutes each side.

5

Sauces

may be prepared and

kept hot in a Pyrex jug in the simmering oven covered with cling film. The pan can then be washed and put away, minimising the pans to wash by hand once your guests arrive.

6

Poppadums

can be cooked directly on the boiling plate with the lid lowered for 30 seconds, and without the grease associated with frying. Watch carefully so they don't burn.

7

When making **pancakes,** cook the first side in the usual way in a pan on the boiling plate, but then flip it over to cook the second side on the lightly greased simmering plate. You can then start another pancake in your pan, and **double** your production **speed.**

8

Keep a supply of bright stickers or **Post-it® notes** by your Aga. If you think you might forget something cooking in an oven, place one on the oven door as a visual reminder.

9

Revive a loaf of slightly **stale bread.**

Cut off a slice from the 'open' end of the loaf and discard. Hold the loaf, cut-side down, for a few moments under a running cold tap, and then place in the roasting oven for four minutes for warm, crusty bread.

10

The secret to a **perfect**

Hollandaise

is to place the pan on the black top plate in front of and between the closed lids. The gentle heat is just right and the sauce will not separate.

11

Because Aga ovens are vented, you won't always smell when something is ready. Invest in an **oven timer** you can carry with you, in your pocket or clipped to your clothing, and you will always know when something needs checking.

12

Leave **jars of jam** or syrup for 30 minutes on the back of the top plate of the Aga, with their lids loosened, to **soften** for easy spreading when baking.

13

Whatever the weather bring a touch of the Mediterranean to your kitchen with your very own **sun-dried** style **tomatoes.**

Slice them, season well, and leave to dry out on racks in the simmering or warming ovens.

14

The knack to **cleaning**
hot plate lids

is to leave them up for a while to cool down a little. Then place the cold plain shelf on top of an Aga grill rack or toaster, placed on the hotplate, to protect yourself from the heat while cleaning inside the lids.

15

Keep your freezer stocked with half-baked petits pains and twelve-inch baguettes. In just eight minutes in the middle of the roasting oven, these will bake from frozen.

An instant supply of warm bread

for an impromptu lunch.

16

Keep **just-cooked roast potatoes**

warm without making them soggy. Place the filled ovenproof serving dish on the Aga toaster on the floor of the roasting oven, with a cold plain shelf above to prevent them over-browning.

17

Stale white bread will make

wonderful dried breadcrumbs.

Discard all the crusts and blitz them in a food processor, then dry out on a tray on the top of the cooker overnight.

18

To clean your Aga

use Aga cleaning paste. Rub it on all over the enamel and leave it for a good five to ten minutes. Then wipe it off along with all the dirt. But don't use it on the chrome lids – a soapy cloth and dry towel are best here.

19

To loosen tight metal **screw-top jars,**

simply place the lid side down on the simmering plate for 30 seconds. The metal lid expands and then is easily twisted off using a cloth.

20

Keep a lined Swiss Roll tin ready in your cupboard so you can make a

quick cake

in the time it takes a kettle to boil. Seven minutes later, turn out, fill, and roll up for a perfect ten-minute store-cupboard cake.

21

Bread dough

will prove brilliantly if the bowl is placed
on a work surface next to the Aga.
And for the final rise leave the bread tins
on a trivet on the top plate.

22

When baking bread throw a tablespoonful of water onto the floor of the oven just before shutting the oven door.
The steam produced will ensure

a perfect crust.

23

To safely **air laundry,**

fold it up and place it on top of the simmering plate lid. Don't use the boiling plate lid or you will risk scorching.

24

Keep a mug of **coffee hot** whilst chatting on the phone by leaving it on the top plate in front of and between the lids.

25

To fry eggs

without using a frying pan, use a piece of Bake-O-Glide placed on the simmering plate. Crack the egg into the centre of the sheet, and lower the lid to speed up the cooking. Fat-free and no washing-up.

26

For pizzas to die for,

cook directly on the floor of the roasting oven. Keep the oven floor clean by brushing out with a wire brush. Vacuum out when the cooker is being serviced.

27

Cook **fruit for marmalade**

in the simmering oven, then add sugar preheated in the roasting oven for five minutes, before boiling for a set on the boiling plate. Sterilise the jars in the simmering oven before filling.

28

To protect your arms

when reaching into the depths of the hot ovens, invest in an Aga gauntlet. The clever design features a unique grease and steam barrier layer.

29

Candlesticks marked with candle wax?

Place them on a sheet of cardboard in a tin on the floor of the simmering oven. The gentle warmth will melt the wax and it will run off and soak into the cardboard. Then simply buff to a shine with a soft, dry cloth.

30

Try **roasting** your own **chestnuts** in the roasting oven. Cut an 'X' on the curved side with a sharp paring knife, place them on a roasting tin and sprinkle with a few teaspoons of water. Roast on the grid shelf on the floor of the oven for up to 40 minutes. You will need to enlist help to peel while they are still warm.

31

For almost **instant drop scones,**

keep the sieved dry ingredients ready-weighed out in an airtight container. When hungry friends drop by, just add an egg and some milk and you can offer them piping hot scones in less than two minutes.

32

Keep a warm plate on a folded tea towel on the closed boiling plate lid when making drop scones, Welshcakes, pikelets and crumpets. You can build up a supply of freshly made fare to

keep hot

while you finish the batch, covering with the end of the tea towel to prevent them drying out.

33

If cooking something on the hot plate which will splash or spit a lot, prop the cold plain shelf up against the open lid to

protect from mess.

Wherever possible cook messy foods in the roasting oven.

34

Dry your own **herbs**

by placing them overnight on cake cooling racks on a cloth on top of the simmering plate lid. Once thoroughly dry, crumble and store in clean airtight jars in a cool dark place.

35

Make **fat-free croûtons**

for garnishing soups and salads by dicing bread and crisping in the simmering oven.

36

Aga-baked potatoes are a revelation, and cooking just one is no extravagance. Prick and cook for 1-1½ hours on the grid shelf on the lowest set of runners in the roasting oven. For more than a dozen, allow a longer cooking time.

37

Try **roasting** your own **coffee beans.**

Spread a thin layer in a cast iron pan, and place on the floor of the roasting oven for 10-15 minutes. Shake the pan every so often. To remove the husks shake the cooled beans in a sieve, then keep refrigerated or frozen in a sealed container until required for grinding.

38

Make your own Aga roller towel using popper fastenings or Velcro, and fit over the Aga rail for a

warm, dry hand towel

that never falls off.

39

To dry out wet shoes,

football boots and trainers, hang them over the Aga rail by tying their laces together.

40

Always **keep your plain shelf cold**

and stored away from the Aga. This can then be placed on runners above any food which is browning too quickly in the roasting oven. It must be cold to have this shielding effect.

41

The full-size Aga roasting tin or baking tray may also be used like a cold plain shelf to

protect food **from browning,**

if your plain shelf is already in use.

42

Dry awkward-shaped metal cooking **utensils** and kitchen gadgets, graters, etc., on the warm top plate so they don't go rusty in storage.

43

Use the gentle warmth of the top of the Aga to **soften, melt or warm** ingredients for cooking. Soften butter, melt chocolate and warm bread flour in the bowl for brilliant bread making.

44

For most foods cooked in the simmering oven, pans should be covered with

well-fitting lids.

However, long slow-cooked Ragù-type sauces can be left uncovered to reduce.

45

Always preheat the Aga toaster
on the hotplate before making

toast to **avoid**

any danger of **sticking.**

Clean only with the wire brush.

46

If you are **in a hurry for breakfast,**

boil the kettle on the boiling plate at the same time as making toast directly on the simmering plate.

47

For **juicy cobs of sweetcorn**

cooked to perfection, keep in their husks and soak in cold water for 5 minutes before wrapping tightly in foil and placing onto a tray on the grid shelf on the floor of the roasting oven. They will take between 15-20 minutes. To serve with them, simply soften some butter in a dish on the top plate.

48

If you have an open fire, **dry** out **kindling** for it in the simmering or warming ovens. Be creative – dried-out orange peel makes excellent tinder!

49

To minimise mess when using the ridged Aga griller, preheat it first dry for four minutes on the boiling plate, lightly rub the ridges with a small piece of fat from the side of the meat, then add the meat and cook on the floor of the roasting oven, turning once. This saves a lot of splatters on the top plate.

50

In the depths of winter, warm your hats, scarves and mittens on the top of the Aga before braving the elements. Post-sledging clothing can also be quickly dried off on the Aga.

Richard Maggs

A dynamic and accomplished chef,
Richard is an authority on Aga cookery.
As well as having featured on TV and radio,
he has written for several food magazines
including the official Aga Magazine.
He is also the resident Aga cookery expert,
The Cookery Doctor, with the award-winning
Agalinks website at www.agalinks.com.

A selected list of Aga titles from Absolute Press

All titles are available to order. Send cheques, made payable to Absolute Press, or VISA/Mastercard details to Absolute Press, Scarborough House, 29 James Street West, Bath BA1 2BT. Phone 01225 316 013 for any further details.

Tim James
Aga: The Story of a Kitchen Classic
The beautifully illustrated, definitive 80-year history of a kitchen icon, told through the memories of friends and family of its Nobel prize-winning inventor; through the stories of those who manufactured it and in the words of those who own it, including Jamie Oliver and Jilly Cooper. (£30)

Louise Walker's *Traditional Aga* titles
Louise Walker has become a guru for Aga owners.
Her bestselling Traditional Aga *titles are packed with simple, stunning recipes. This is an essential series for every Aga cook.*

The Traditional Aga Cookery Book (£9.95)
The Traditional Aga Party Book (£9.95)
The Traditional Aga Book of Slow Cooking (£9.95)
The Traditional Aga Box Set (*all three titles above*) (£29.50)

The Traditional Aga Four Seasons Cookery Book (£9.95)
The Traditional Aga Book of Vegetarian Cooking (£9.95)
The Traditional Aga Book of Bread & Cakes (£9.95)
The Traditional Aga Box Set 2 (*all three titles above*) (£29.50)